Mrs. Pyle

THIS BOOK IS
ESPECIALLY FOR...

Mrs. Pyle

WHERE'S CUPID?

By
Anthony Tallarico

Copyright © 1992 Kidsbooks Inc. and Anthony Tallarico
7004 N. California Ave.
Chicago, IL 60645

Beware! If you get hit by one of my arrows you may fall in love, just like these couples.

FIND CUPID AMONG THESE CARTOON FAVORITES AND…

- ☐ Balloons (4)
- ☐ Banana peel
- ☐ Baseball
- ☐ Basket
- ☐ Beehive
- ☐ Bone
- ☐ Book
- ☐ Bottle
- ☐ Cactus
- ☐ Candle
- ☐ Cheese
- ☐ Cup
- ☐ Feather
- ☐ Flowers (2)
- ☐ Flying bats (2)
- ☐ Football
- ☐ Hammer
- ☐ Hearts (9)
- ☐ Hose
- ☐ Jack-o'-lanterns (2)
- ☐ Kites (2)
- ☐ Lock
- ☐ Magic lamp
- ☐ Mirror
- ☐ Mushroom
- ☐ Music note
- ☐ Painted egg
- ☐ Periscope
- ☐ Piggy bank
- ☐ Pirate
- ☐ Pizzas (2)
- ☐ Purse
- ☐ Rock
- ☐ Tinkerbell
- ☐ Tire
- ☐ Top hat
- ☐ Turtle
- ☐ Umbrella

Who is going to a barn dance?
Who has peanuts?
Who is wearing earrings?

You must have heard of Romeo and Juliet. Well, they didn't even like each other until I appeared on the scene!

SEARCH FOR CUPID IN VERONA AND...

- ☐ Baseball cap
- ☐ Bird
- ☐ Bucket
- ☐ Bull's-eye
- ☐ Candy cane
- ☐ Duck
- ☐ Envelope
- ☐ Escaped convict
- ☐ Fire hydrant
- ☐ Fish (2)
- ☐ Fishing pole
- ☐ Football player
- ☐ Friar
- ☐ Frog
- ☐ Hamburger
- ☐ Hot dog
- ☐ Ice-cream cone
- ☐ Key
- ☐ Kites (2)
- ☐ Light bulb
- ☐ Mouse
- ☐ Paper airplane
- ☐ Pie
- ☐ Pig
- ☐ Pillow
- ☐ Pizza slice
- ☐ Propeller
- ☐ Rabbit
- ☐ Roller skates
- ☐ Sailboat
- ☐ Saw
- ☐ Skateboard
- ☐ Skull
- ☐ Sock
- ☐ Stars (3)
- ☐ Straw
- ☐ Sunglasses
- ☐ Sword
- ☐ TV set
- ☐ Worm

Who doesn't know his math?
What are the names of the streets?

Tom Sawyer met his sweetheart Becky and it was love at first sight. Thanks to me, that is!

LOOK FOR CUPID IN THIS SPOOKY CAVE AND…

- ☐ Apple core
- ☐ Balloons (2)
- ☐ Barrel
- ☐ Baseball bat
- ☐ Bell
- ☐ Boat
- ☐ Bones (4)
- ☐ Boot
- ☐ Briefcase
- ☐ Broom
- ☐ Brush
- ☐ Candle
- ☐ Crayon
- ☐ Cup
- ☐ Dogs (2)
- ☐ Drum
- ☐ Envelope
- ☐ Flowers (3)
- ☐ Football
- ☐ Ghosts (3)
- ☐ Hearts (2)
- ☐ Helmets (2)
- ☐ Kite
- ☐ Little Red Riding Hood
- ☐ Monsters with horns (4)
- ☐ Mouse
- ☐ Mummy
- ☐ Painted eggs (2)
- ☐ Piggy bank
- ☐ Ring
- ☐ Skulls (2)
- ☐ Snake
- ☐ Sock
- ☐ Straw
- ☐ Tent
- ☐ Tic-tac-toe
- ☐ Tire
- ☐ Top hat
- ☐ Train engine
- ☐ Turtle
- ☐ Umbrella

Who is looking for her eggs?
Who ate the apple?

When George Washington married his wife Martha, I was there!

FIND CUPID AT WASHINGTON'S WEDDING AND...

- ☐ Apple
- ☐ Balloon
- ☐ Banana peel
- ☐ Bone
- ☐ Bonnet
- ☐ Bowling ball
- ☐ Bucket
- ☐ Butterfly
- ☐ Camera
- ☐ Candy cane
- ☐ Chalkboard
- ☐ Crayon
- ☐ Drumstick
- ☐ Egg
- ☐ Feathers (4)
- ☐ Firecracker
- ☐ Fish (2)
- ☐ Ghost
- ☐ Hearts (4)
- ☐ Kites (2)
- ☐ Knight
- ☐ Mouse
- ☐ Mushroom
- ☐ Pencil
- ☐ Pizza
- ☐ Rabbits (2)
- ☐ Seal
- ☐ Shovel
- ☐ Snail
- ☐ Socks (3)
- ☐ Stool
- ☐ Stump of a
  cherry tree
- ☐ Surfboard
- ☐ Toaster
- ☐ Trumpet
- ☐ Turtle
- ☐ Umbrella
- ☐ Witch's hats (2)
- ☐ Worm

Who wasn't invited?
Who forgot to bring
  the rice?
When did Washington
  become president?

Christopher's sweetheart said a sad farewell when Columbus set sail in 1492.

HUNT FOR CUPID AT THE CROWDED HARBOR AND...

☐ Ball
☐ Barrel
☐ Baseball cap
☐ Beach chair
☐ Bottle
☐ Candles (3)
☐ Chef
☐ Clothespins (2)
☐ Diving board
☐ Dogs (2)
☐ Fish
☐ Flag
☐ Football player
☐ Ghost
☐ Hearts (3)
☐ Horse
☐ Hot dog
☐ Hourglass
☐ Jack-o'-lantern
☐ Lost boot
☐ Mermaids (2)
☐ Mouse
☐ Octopus
☐ Paper airplane
☐ Periscope
☐ Pig
☐ Pillow
☐ Policeman
☐ Rowboats (3)
☐ Skier
☐ Snowman
☐ Starfish
☐ Surfer
☐ Sword
☐ Telescope
☐ Tire
☐ TV antenna
☐ Wooden leg
☐ Zipper

What is the king's name?
What is the bull's name?

My arrow caused Robin Hood to fall for Maid Marian, and she fell for him, too!

SEARCH FOR CUPID IN SHERWOOD FOREST AND...

☐ Apple
☐ Balloon
☐ Bell
☐ Birdcage
☐ Broom
☐ Brush
☐ Cactus
☐ Camel
☐ Candle
☐ Car
☐ Clock
☐ Crown
☐ Cup
☐ Eagle
☐ Elephant
☐ Feathers (3)
☐ Fish (2)
☐ Fishing pole
☐ Fork
☐ Ghosts (2)
☐ Gold coin
☐ Golf club
☐ Hearts (5)
☐ Humpty Dumpty
☐ Igloo
☐ Kites (2)
☐ Ladder
☐ Mice (2)
☐ Oilcan
☐ Owl
☐ Pie
☐ Pizza
☐ Scarf
☐ Shovel
☐ Slingshot
☐ Snake
☐ Star
☐ Sunglasses
☐ Turtles (3)

Where is Little John?
Where is Friar Tuck?

By the shores of Gitche-Gumee I shot my arrows at both Hiawatha and the lovely Minnehaha.

LOOK FOR CUPID IN THIS INDIAN CAMP AND...

- ☐ Ant
- ☐ Apple
- ☐ Basket of corn
- ☐ Baseball bats
- ☐ Bears (2)
- ☐ Beaver
- ☐ Bone
- ☐ Buffalo
- ☐ Canoe
- ☐ Cat
- ☐ Deer
- ☐ Dog
- ☐ Drum
- ☐ Duck
- ☐ Eagle
- ☐ Fish (5)
- ☐ Frog
- ☐ Ghost
- ☐ Guitar
- ☐ Hearts (14)
- ☐ Moose
- ☐ Mouse
- ☐ Owls (2)
- ☐ Pencil
- ☐ Pig
- ☐ Pony
- ☐ Porcupine
- ☐ Rabbits (3)
- ☐ Skunk
- ☐ Snake in the grass
- ☐ Snake out of the grass
- ☐ Spacecraft
- ☐ Sunflower
- ☐ Tomahawk
- ☐ Turkey
- ☐ Turtle
- ☐ Windup cowboy
- ☐ Wolf
- ☐ Worm

What do you call an Indian tent?
Where is Gitche-Gumee?

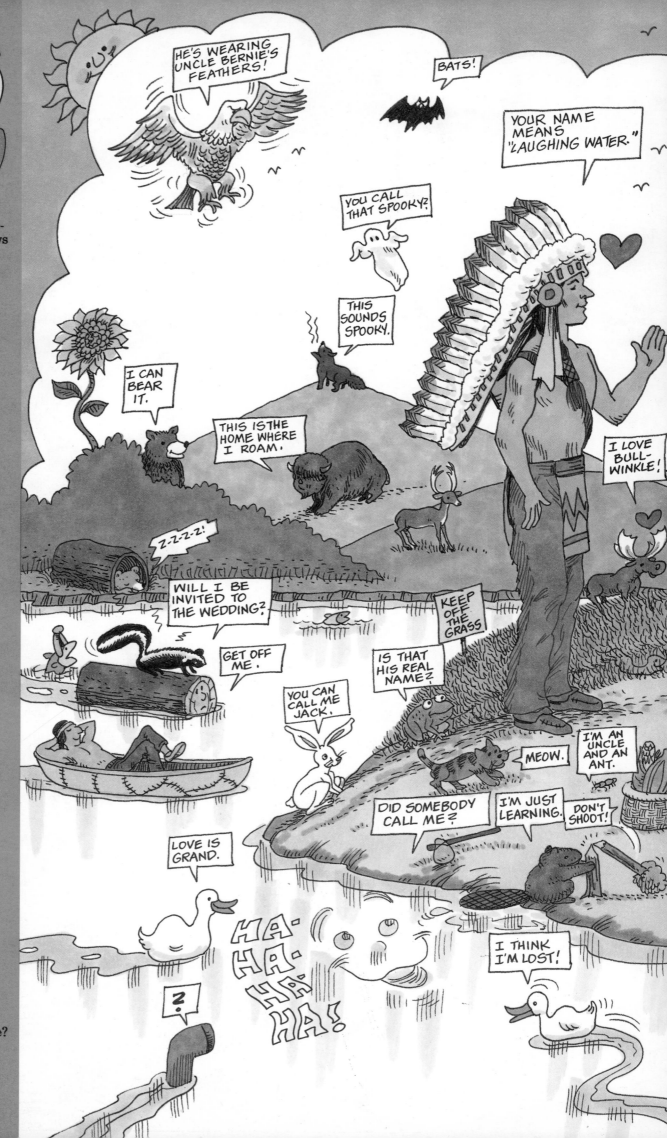

Sometimes my arrow caused strange reactions, like with Quasimodo, the Hunchback of Notre Dame ... or was it Yale or U.C.L.A.?

FIND CUPID ON THIS BUSY STREET AND...

- ☐ Banana peel
- ☐ Barrel
- ☐ Basketball hoop
- ☐ Black cat
- ☐ Boat builder
- ☐ Bones (3)
- ☐ Bowling ball
- ☐ Candle
- ☐ Candy cane
- ☐ Chef
- ☐ Crown
- ☐ Firefighter
- ☐ Football player
- ☐ Ghost
- ☐ Goat
- ☐ Green wagon
- ☐ Hearts (4)
- ☐ Horses (2)
- ☐ Key
- ☐ Ladder
- ☐ Laundry
- ☐ Mouse
- ☐ Music note
- ☐ Newspaper
- ☐ Panda
- ☐ Pig
- ☐ Pitchfork
- ☐ Pole vaulter
- ☐ Record player
- ☐ Red balloon
- ☐ Santa Claus
- ☐ Skateboard
- ☐ Sword
- ☐ Top hat
- ☐ Torch
- ☐ Umbrellas (2)

What is the girl's name?
What's cooking?
What time is it?'

It was my doing that brought Davy Crockett and his wife Polly together.

HUNT FOR CUPID IN THE CROCKETT'S YARD AND...

☐ Apple
☐ Axe
☐ Ball
☐ Baskets (2)
☐ Bears (3)
☐ Bee
☐ Beaver
☐ Broom
☐ Bucket
☐ Carrot
☐ Chicken
☐ Child's wagon
☐ Covered wagon
☐ Cow bell
☐ Cricket
☐ Deer (2)
☐ Dogs (2)
☐ Goldilocks
☐ Hearts (3)
☐ Horseshoes
☐ Lion
☐ Little Red
    Riding Hood
☐ Lost hat
☐ Moose
☐ Owl
☐ Pinocchio
☐ Rabbits (2)
☐ Rain barrel
☐ Rake
☐ Shovel
☐ Snake
☐ Spinning wheel
☐ Squirrel
☐ Tin man
☐ Tugboat
☐ Turkey
☐ Wagon wheel

Where is Davy going? Who is looking for the three bears?

I set it all up for Frankenstein's monster to meet his bride!

FIND CUPID AMONG THESE GRUESOME GHOULIES AND…

- ☐ Baseball bat
- ☐ Baseball cap
- ☐ Bird's nest
- ☐ Blue moon
- ☐ Bones (2)
- ☐ Broken TV set
- ☐ Candles (3)
- ☐ Chef's hat
- ☐ Count Dracula
- ☐ Eyeglasses (2)
- ☐ Flowers (3)
- ☐ Ghosts (4)
- ☐ Hammer
- ☐ Hearts (4)
- ☐ Hockey stick
- ☐ Jack-o´-lanterns (2)
- ☐ Key
- ☐ King Kong
- ☐ Lollipop
- ☐ Mitten
- ☐ Mouse
- ☐ Musician
- ☐ Octopus
- ☐ Paper airplane
- ☐ Piggy bank
- ☐ Pyramid
- ☐ Rabbit
- ☐ Roller skates
- ☐ Sailor's cap
- ☐ Sled
- ☐ Sock
- ☐ Straw
- ☐ Straw hat
- ☐ Tent
- ☐ Turtle
- ☐ Two-headed monster
- ☐ Watering can
- ☐ Worms (2)

Where did the hot air balloon come from?
Who has the rice?

Sometimes my arrows didn't work as I planned them to. An example of this is Ichabod Crane and Katrina Van Tassel.

LOOK FOR CUPID ON THIS MOONLIT NIGHT AND...

- ☐ Arrows (2)
- ☐ Axe
- ☐ Bearded man
- ☐ Bell
- ☐ Bone
- ☐ Book
- ☐ Bowling ball
- ☐ Broken heart
- ☐ Broom
- ☐ Comb
- ☐ Cradle
- ☐ Dog
- ☐ Fish
- ☐ Flying bat
- ☐ Frying pan
- ☐ Horseshoe
- ☐ Hot dog
- ☐ Knight
- ☐ Lost boot
- ☐ Owl
- ☐ Pencil
- ☐ Periscope
- ☐ Pie
- ☐ Pig
- ☐ Rabbit
- ☐ Santa Claus
- ☐ Scarecrow
- ☐ Scissors
- ☐ Skateboard
- ☐ Snail
- ☐ Squirrel
- ☐ Telescope
- ☐ Toothbrush
- ☐ Top hat
- ☐ Unicorn
- ☐ Worm

What is the real name of the headless horseman? What was Ichabod's job?

Poor Rip Van Winkle! Sometimes I wish I hadn't shot my arrow at him at all!

SEARCH FOR CUPID AMONG THE FALLING LEAVES AND…

- ☐ Ball of yarn
- ☐ Balloon
- ☐ Banana peel
- ☐ Bat under a hat
- ☐ Birdhouse
- ☐ Bone
- ☐ Bottle
- ☐ Broken dish
- ☐ Butterfly
- ☐ Cat
- ☐ Crayon
- ☐ Drum
- ☐ Duck
- ☐ Fish (2)
- ☐ Fishing pole
- ☐ Football player
- ☐ Golf ball
- ☐ Goose
- ☐ Hammer
- ☐ Hearts (2)
- ☐ Hoe
- ☐ Igloo
- ☐ Kettles (2)
- ☐ Key
- ☐ Knife
- ☐ Ladder
- ☐ Moose
- ☐ Paper airplane
- ☐ Pigs (2)
- ☐ Pitchfork
- ☐ Pumpkin
- ☐ Rat in a cap
- ☐ Skateboard
- ☐ Spoon
- ☐ Swing
- ☐ Turtle
- ☐ Umpire
- ☐ Wished-out wishing well
- ☐ Worm

What is Rip's dog's name?
How long did Rip sleep?

I'm out to get you, too! Look for your name here, but if I missed it, write it in one of the blank hearts yourself. Fill in your friend's names, too!

FIND CUPID AMONG THE HEARTS AND FLOWERS AND…

- ☐ Apple
- ☐ Arrows (3)
- ☐ Balloons (3)
- ☐ Barbell
- ☐ Baseball cap
- ☐ Birds (3)
- ☐ Butterfly
- ☐ Carrot
- ☐ Chimney
- ☐ Cup
- ☐ Cupcake
- ☐ Fish
- ☐ Football
- ☐ Ice-cream cone
- ☐ Kite
- ☐ Lips
- ☐ Magnifying glass
- ☐ Music notes (3)
- ☐ Paintbrush
- ☐ Pizza slice
- ☐ Rabbit
- ☐ Ring
- ☐ Scarf
- ☐ Seal
- ☐ Snake
- ☐ Spray can
- ☐ Star
- ☐ Tent
- ☐ Tepee
- ☐ Top hat
- ☐ Traffic signal
- ☐ Tulip
- ☐ Umbrella
- ☐ Watermelon slice

What time is it?

Cupid has shot an arrow at all of your "Where Are They?" friends. Find the 16 arrows and…

☐ Balloons (2)
☐ Bone
☐ Flowers (12)
☐ Moon face
☐ Mouse
☐ Stars (5)
☐ Wreath